T0413959

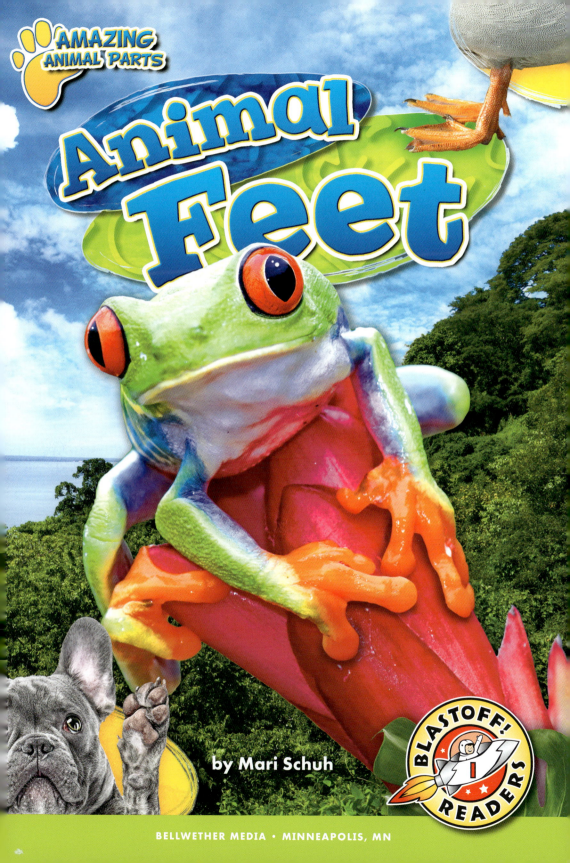

Animal Feet

by Mari Schuh

BLASTOFF!
READERS

BELLWETHER MEDIA • MINNEAPOLIS, MN

Blastoff! Readers are carefully developed by literacy experts to build reading stamina and move students toward fluency by combining standards-based content with developmentally appropriate text.

Level 1 provides the most support through repetition of high-frequency words, light text, predictable sentence patterns, and strong visual support.

Level 2 offers early readers a bit more challenge through varied sentences, increased text load, and text-supportive special features.

Level 3 advances early-fluent readers toward fluency through increased text load, less reliance on photos, advancing concepts, longer sentences, and more complex special features.

★ **Blastoff! Universe**

Reading Level

Grade
K

Grades
1–3

Grade
4

This edition first published in 2024 by Bellwether Media, Inc.

No part of this publication may be reproduced in whole or in part without written permission of the publisher. For information regarding permission, write to Bellwether Media, Inc., Attention: Permissions Department, 6012 Blue Circle Drive, Minnetonka, MN 55343.

Library of Congress Cataloging-in-Publication Data

LC record for Animal Feet available at: https://lccn.loc.gov/2023039752

Text copyright © 2024 by Bellwether Media, Inc. BLASTOFF! READERS and associated logos are trademarks and/or registered trademarks of Bellwether Media, Inc.

Editor: Rebecca Sabelko   Designer: Andrea Schneider

Printed in the United States of America, North Mankato, MN.

Table of Contents

Helpful Feet

Animals have different kinds of feet. Feet help animals move!

Webbed Feet

Ducks have **webbed** feet. Their feet look like **paddles**.

webbed
feet

Webbed feet
help ducks move.
They push water
so ducks can swim.

How Webbed Feet Work

duck moves forward →

← webbed feet push water back

Sticky Feet

There are many different tree frogs. All of them have sticky feet!

tree frog
foot

11

Tree frogs hide from **predators** in trees. The frogs use their sticky feet to climb.

predator

13

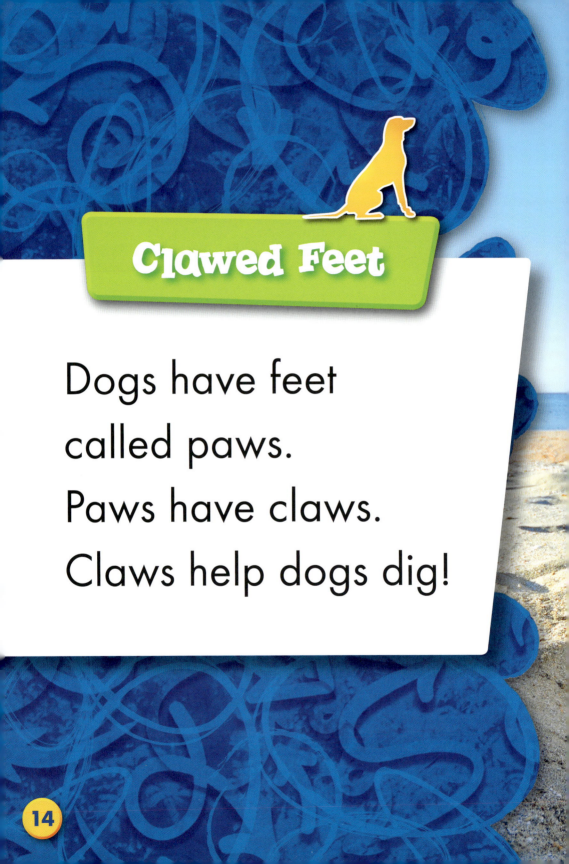

Clawed Feet

Dogs have feet
called paws.
Paws have claws.
Claws help dogs dig!

claws

paw →

15

Paws have thick pads.
Pads **protect**
small bones
in dogs' feet.

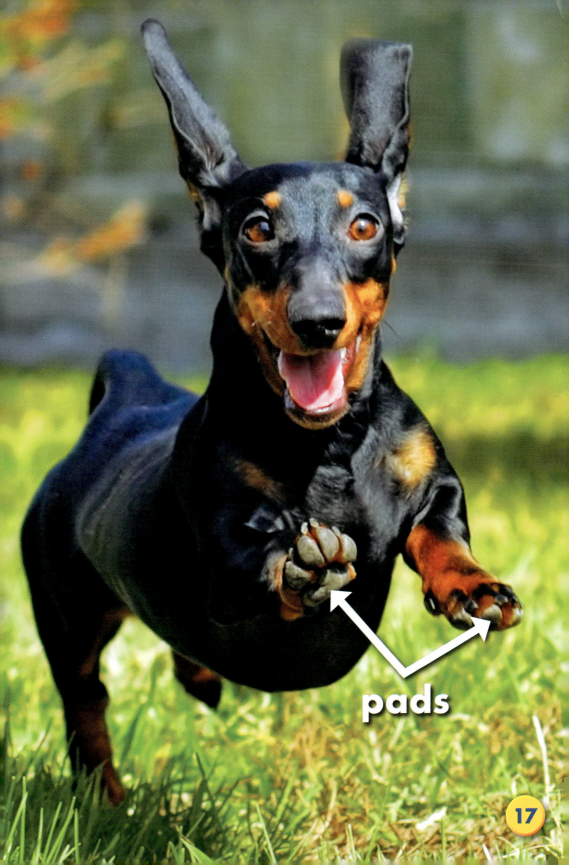

pads

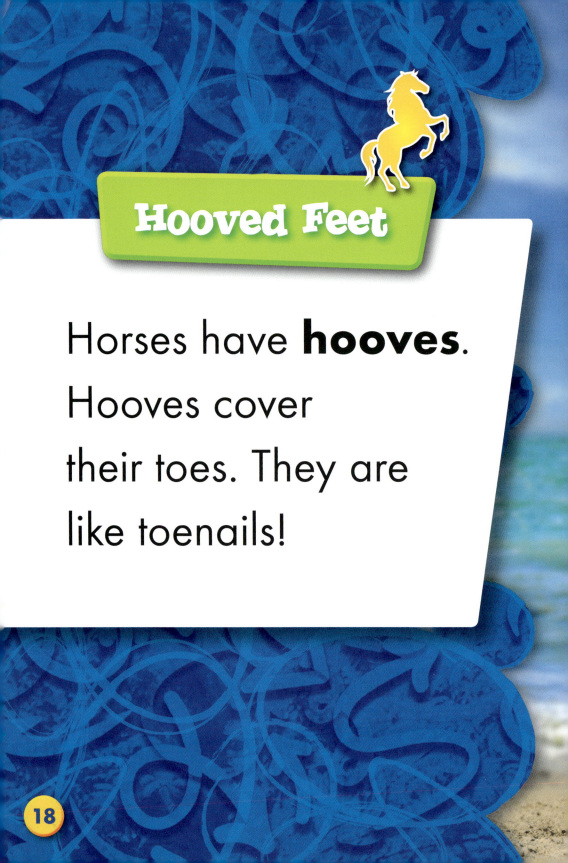

Hooved Feet

Horses have **hooves**. Hooves cover their toes. They are like toenails!

More Hooves!

two toes — goat

three toes — rhino

four toes — pig

one toe

Hooves protect horses' toes. Horses can run and play!

Glossary

hooves

hard coverings that protect the feet of some animals

protect

to keep safe

paddles

flat tools used to move and steer small boats

webbed

having a bit of skin between the fingers or toes

predators

animals that hunt other animals for food

To Learn More

AT THE LIBRARY

Culliford, Amy. *Feet*. New York, N.Y.: Crabtree Publishing Company, 2022.

Griffin, Mary. *Whose Feet Are Those?* New York, N.Y.: Gareth Stevens Publishing, 2024.

Rathburn, Betsy. *Baby Horses*. Minneapolis, Minn.: Bellwether Media, 2022.

ON THE WEB

FACTSURFER

Factsurfer.com gives you a safe, fun way to find more information.

1. Go to www.factsurfer.com.

2. Enter "animal feet" into the search box and click 🔍.

3. Select your book cover to see a list of related content.

Index